D0318943

Rebecca Hunter

Raintree

www.raintreepublishers.co.uk
Visit our website to find out more information about **Raintree** books.

To order:
☎ Phone 44 (0) 1865 888112
▤ Send a fax to 44 (0) 1865 314091
▢ Visit the Raintree Bookshop at www.raintreepublishers.co.uk to browse our catalogue and order online.

First published in Great Britain by Raintree,
Halley Court, Jordan Hill, Oxford
OX2 8EJ, part of Harcourt Education.

Raintree is a registered trademark of Harcourt
Education Ltd.

Produced for Raintree by Discovery Books Ltd
Design: Ian Winton
Editorial: Rebecca Hunter
Consultant: Jeremy Bloomfield
Commissioned Photography: Chris Fairclough
Illustrations: Keith Williams, Jenny Mumford
and Stefan Chabluk
Production: Jonathan Smith

Originated by Dot Gradations Ltd
Printed and bound in China by South China
  Printing Company

ISBN 1 844 21569 5 (hardback)
07 06 05 04 03
10 9 8 7 6 5 4 3 2 1

ISBN 1 844 21576 8 (paperback)
08 07 06 05 04
10 9 8 7 6 5 4 3 2 1

British Library Cataloguing in Publication Data
Hunter, Rebecca
Light and Dark. – (Discovering Science)
535

A full catalogue record for this book is available from the
British Library.

Acknowledgements
The publishers would like to thank the following for
permission to reproduce photographs:
Bruce Coleman: page **21**, top (Tore Hagman), **24** (both),
25, top, **27** (Jane Burton), **28** (Peter A Hinchliffe);
Discovery Picture Library: page **10**, **12** bottom, **13** top,
15 top, **17** top; NASA: page **7**, **21** bottom; Oxford
Scientific Films: page **15** bottom (Javed Jafferji), **25**
bottom (Doug Allen), **26** top (Owen Newman), bottom
(Rafi Ben-Shahar); Science Photo Library: page **4** bottom
(Tony Craddock), **5**, European Space Agency, **6** (George
Post), **8** (Brenda Tharp), **9** (Francoise Sauze), **11** (Sheila
Terry), **12**, top (David Nunuk), **14**, bottom (Tek Image),
18 (David Parker), **19** (David Nunuk), **20** bottom (Pascal
Nieto), **22** (Tony Craddock), **29** top (Cordelia Molloy);
gettyimages: page **4**, top (Jerome Tisne), **13** bottom (Jay S
Simon), **14** top (Yvette Cardozo), **17** bottom (Steven
Peters), **29** bottom (Jean-Marc Truchet).

Cover photograph of prism splitting light reproduced
with permission of Science Photo Library.

The publishers would like to thank the following schools
for their help in providing equipment, models and
locations for photography sessions: Bedstone College,
Bucknell, Moor Park, Ludlow and Packwood Haugh,
Shrewsbury.

Every effort has been made to contact copyright holders
of any material reproduced in this book.
Any omissions will be rectified in subsequent printings if
notice is given to the publishers.

Any words appearing in the text in bold, **like
this**, are explained in the Glossary.

CONTENTS

WHAT IS LIGHT?

Light is something that we use and depend on every day, but we do not often stop and think about what light is. Light is really a form of energy that we can see.

▶ *Sunglasses protect your eyes from bright light.*

▼ *Sunlight is what makes plants grow on Earth.*

SUNLIGHT

Most of our light comes from the Sun. Although it is 150 million kilometres (about 93 million miles) away from Earth, the Sun is our nearest star. It gives off huge amounts of energy in the form of heat and light. Some of this energy reaches us on Earth. Without sunlight Earth would be a cold, dark place. Nothing would live here.

The Sun is a huge ball of very hot gases.

DAYLIGHT AND DARKNESS

Earth spins around once every 24 hours. At any one time, half of Earth is in sunlight, and the other half is in darkness. On the light side it is daytime. On the dark side it is night-time. When you have daytime, it will always be night-time on the other side of the world!

The other side of Earth is in darkness.

The Sun lights up one side of Earth.

Because Earth is always turning, the Sun is always setting somewhere, and at the same time rising somewhere else.

SOLAR ECLIPSE

Earth orbits, or travels around, the Sun. The Moon orbits Earth. Sometimes Earth, the Moon and Sun line up so that the Moon is between the Sun and Earth. This causes a solar eclipse. The Sun is about 400 times bigger than the Moon, but it is also about 400 times further away from Earth. So the Sun and Moon appear to be the same size to us.

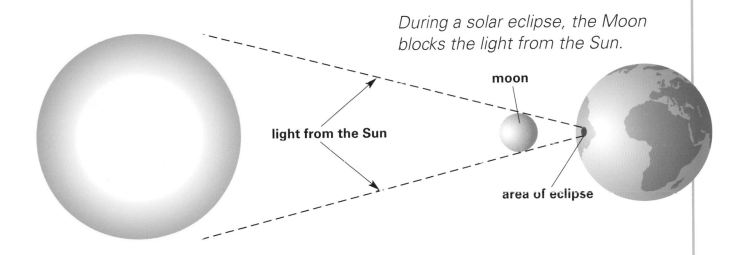

During a solar eclipse, the Moon blocks the light from the Sun.

moon

light from the Sun

area of eclipse

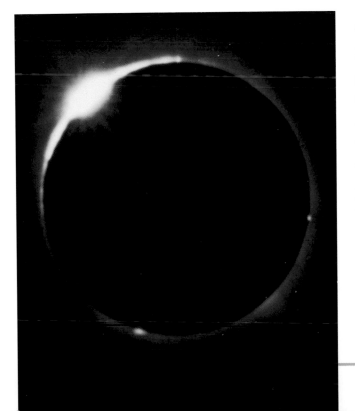

As the Moon passes in front of the Sun, almost all of the sunlight is blocked. Then a small area on the Earth becomes dark. The darkness lasts only a few minutes, but many animals believe it is sunset and try to go to sleep!

The Moon blocks nearly all the light from the Sun in a solar eclipse.

PROPERTIES OF LIGHT

LIGHT RAYS

Light travels in straight lines. You can see this when sunlight is streaming through a window, or when light shines through the trees in a forest. Car headlights shine a beam of light straight ahead. These lines of light are called light rays.

PROJECT

This experiment shows how light travels in straight lines.

You will need:
a torch
an old shoebox
talcum powder.

1. Make a small hole in one end of the shoebox.

2. Put the torch inside the box.

3. Turn the lights off and the torch on. Sprinkle some talcum powder into the air over the light beam.

4. The powder will make the light rays show up clearly.

THE SPEED OF LIGHT

Light travels very fast. The speed of light is the fastest thing we know. It travels at about 300,000 kilometres (186,000 miles) per second. At this speed, sunlight takes about 8 minutes to reach Earth.

When you watch a firework display, you see the fireworks before you hear them. This is because light travels faster than sound.

Light travels much faster than sound. This is why you see a jet plane before you hear it, or you see lightning before you hear the thunder.

SHADOWS

Because light only travels in straight lines, it cannot bend around objects in its path. Most objects block light. This makes shadows on the other side of the objects. You can see this yourself when you are outside on a sunny day. Wherever you go, you will have a shadow at your feet.

TELLING THE TIME

You can use shadows to tell the time of day. Look at the shadows cast by trees. In the middle of the day, when the sun is high in the sky, the shadows are short. In the early morning and late in the afternoon, the Sun is near the horizon and the shadows are much longer.

early morning

midday

late afternoon

On a sunny day, you can tell the time by using the shadow on a sundial. Sundials are one of the oldest kinds of clocks. Instead of moving hands, they use a shadow cast by the Sun. As time passes, the shadow moves around the dial, and the time of day can be read.

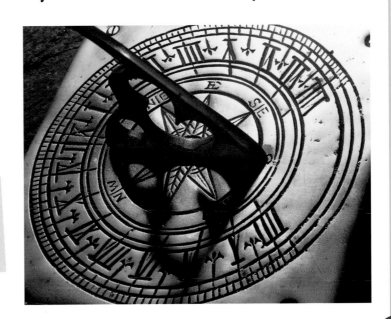

A sundial uses a shadow to tell the time.

IT'S TRUE!

The first sundials were used by the Chinese more than 4000 years ago.

PROJECT

You could make your own sundial.

You will need:
an open space outside
a straight stick
some large pebbles
a watch or clock
a sunny day!

1. Push the stick into the ground.

2. Using the watch to time, mark the position of the stick's shadow with a pebble every hour.

3. Write a number on each pebble for each hour of daylight.

4. You will now be able to tell the time each day by looking at your sundial.

REFLECTED AND BENT LIGHT

REFLECTION

You see some things because they make their own light – like the Sun, a fire, or electric lights. You can also see objects that do not make light – like this book, or a table, or a bird. That is because these things reflect light. When light hits something, it bounces back in all directions. This reflected, or **scattered light**, enters your eyes and allows you to see things around you.

▶ *We can see the Moon because it reflects the Sun's light.*

Some objects reflect light better than others. How well an object reflects light depends on its surface.

This smooth shiny tea service reflects much more light than it would if it were rough or painted black.

MIRRORS

The best surface for reflecting light is a mirror. A mirror reflects nearly all the light that hits it. The surface is so shiny that it gives an almost perfect **image**. This is called a **reflection**. A mirror-image is not an exact copy of the original but a reversed copy. The right side of the object appears on the left in the image.

If you raise your left hand, your reflection will be raising its right hand!

You can see this effect by holding a piece of paper with writing on it up to a mirror. Can you read it?

◀ *When you look at writing in a mirror – its reversed (backwards).*

▶ *The surface of still water can act like a mirror. When the surface of water has ripples, the light is reflected in different directions, and the reflections are blurred.*

SHINING THROUGH

You have seen objects that reflect light and block it, making shadows, but some objects let light pass through them. Things that allow some light to pass through them without letting you see through clearly are called **translucent**.

This igloo is made of translucent ice.

Other things that allow nearly all light to pass through them and that you can see right through clearly are called **transparent**.

This goldfish can be seen easily through the transparent plastic bag.

REFRACTION

When light moves from one transparent material to another, it changes speed, and the light rays bend. This is called **refraction** and is why a brush in a glass of water looks as if it is broken at the point where it enters the water.

Ponds and rock pools are always deeper than they look. This is because light reflected from the water is refracted, or bent, as it leaves the water – making the bottom of the pond seem closer than it really is.

◄ *Spear fishermen must remember refraction of light when they aim for a fish, if they are to be successful.*

LIGHT AND SIGHT

THE EYE

Have you ever wondered how your eyes work? Light from a light source, or reflected off an object, enters through the **pupil** and meets the **lens**. The lens focuses, or directs, the light on to the **retina**. Special cells in the retina send messages to the brain, and the brain tells us what we are seeing.

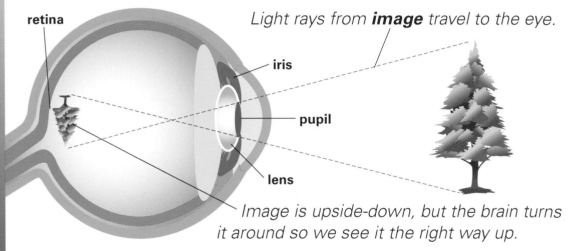

retina

iris

pupil

lens

*Light rays from **image** travel to the eye.*

Image is upside-down, but the brain turns it around so we see it the right way up.

The iris controls how much light enters the eye through the pupil. In bright light, the iris closes the pupil. In dim light, the pupil opens wider. You can easily see how this happens in your own eyes. Stand in front of a mirror in a darkened room. Now get someone to turn on the light. Watch your pupils, and you will see how they quickly shrink. Watch what happens when the light is turned off again.

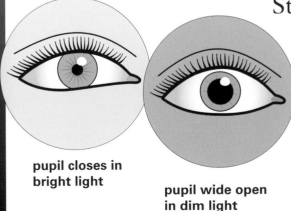

pupil closes in bright light

pupil wide open in dim light

ARTIFICIAL LENSES

We can make lenses out of glass or plastic and use them to help us in many ways. Some people who cannot see well because the lenses in their eyes do not work correctly can improve their sight with these lenses. They can either wear glasses or use **contact lenses** that are worn directly on the eye.

▶ *Glasses come in many shapes and styles.*

Magnifying lenses are used in telescopes to enable us to see things that are far away, such as stars.

LIGHT AND COLOUR

If someone asked you what colour light is, what would you say? You would probably say that light has no colour and that it is objects that have colour.

Actually, sunlight or 'white light', as it is called, is a mixture of colours. This was discovered by Isaac Newton in 1666. He found that if you shone sunlight through a **prism**, it separated out into several colours.

The light that enters a prism is mostly **reflected**, but a small part is **refracted**, or bent, into the six colours of the rainbow: violet, blue, green, yellow, orange and red.

A prism splits white light into the colours of the rainbow.

Rainbows form when sunlight shines through millions of raindrops. As the light passes through each raindrop, it is refracted into the rainbow's colours.

A rainbow is part of a circle of light.

PROJECT

Making rainbows.

You will need:
a strong soap solution made from washing-up liquid and water
a bowl
2–3 tablespoons of sugar
some thin wire that bends.

1. Make up half a bucket of soap solution and add the sugar to it. (This will make the solution thicker.)

2. Bend the wire into a simple shape, leaving a piece of wire as a handle.

3. Dip the shape into the soap solution. Pull it out slowly and look at the rainbow colours.

4. If you make circular shapes, you can try blowing bubbles. You will see a rainbow in the bubbles, too!

REFLECTION OF COLOUR

All objects **absorb**, or soak up, and **reflect** a different range of colours. White objects reflect all colours, which is why they appear white. Black objects absorb all colours, so they appear to have no colour.

A lemon absorbs all colours in sunlight except one – yellow, which it reflects. This is why a lemon looks yellow to us.

▼ *Pigments are chemicals that are added to white paint to give it colour.*

Light is reflected and scattered by almost everything it hits. Tiny **particles** of dust and water in the air scatter blue light more strongly than the other colours, so the sky appears blue to us on Earth.

▶ *When there are no clouds to block the light, the sky appears blue.*

The Moon has no atmosphere to scatter sunlight, so if you were on the Moon the 'sky' would appear black.

Daytime on the Moon. The sky is always black!

LIGHT FOR LIFE

FOOD FROM THE SUN

Plants have an amazing way of making food out of sunlight. This process is called **photosynthesis**. Plants' green leaves allow them to turn the Sun's energy into sugars that they use to grow.

Sunflowers turn to face the Sun. All plants need sunshine.

PROJECT

You could do this experiment to show that plants need light to grow.

You will need:
two pots of compost
some grass seed
an old cardboard box.

1. Plant the grass seed in some compost in the pots. Let it grow on a windowsill until the seedlings are about 3 centimetres high.

2. Now place one pot of grass inside the box, so that it is in darkness.

3. Poke a few holes in the box to give the grass some air.

4. Put the box and the other pot of grass on a windowsill with plenty of light. Water both pots with the same amount of water each day.

5. How do the plants look at the end of a week? What does this tell you about what is needed for plants to grow?

The energy in sunlight that is used by plants is the first stage in the food chain. Plants are eaten by animals, who are in turn eaten by other animals. In this way the energy from the Sun is passed throughout the animal world.

meat eaters

plant eaters

plants

the Sun

23

HUNTERS AND HUNTED

Animals use light to find food and to keep themselves from being eaten. Animals that eat meat have to use their senses of sight, smell and hearing to track down their **prey**. Animals that eat only plants do not have to hunt for their food, but they must keep a sharp look out for **predators**.

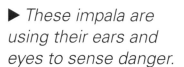

▶ These impala are using their ears and eyes to sense danger.

ATTRACTING AND WARNING COLOURS

Some plants and animals make use of colour to attract other animals towards them, or to warn them to stay away. The bright colours of flowers attract insects that feed on their nectar. While they feed, the insects help **pollinate** the flower.

A colourful butterfly is attracted to a flower by its colour and smell.

Many animals have bright colours that help them attract a mate. Colours can also be a warning to predators. The colourful South American arrow-poison frog is so deadly that the local Indians use the poison on the tips of their arrows. The red and black colouring on a ladybird warns hungry birds that these beetles taste horrible.

The ladybirds' bright colours are a warning to birds.

Colours can also be used as **camouflage** to hide animals. Stripes and spots help break up their outlines, so they can hide among trees or in the grass.

The chameleon is the master of all disguises. With special pigments in its skin, it can change colour to match its surroundings.

IN THE DARK

When there is no light, there is darkness. However, it is almost never completely dark. Even outside at night, the stars provide enough light for many animals to see. **Nocturnal** animals are those that come out at night. They have adapted to life in the dark. Owls have large eyes that are far better than human eyes at seeing in dim light. An owl's eyes are designed to gather as much light as possible.

▶ *An owl can catch a mouse in conditions that we humans would think of as being 'pitch-black'.*

Nocturnal hunters, like lions, have eyes that shine in the dark. They have a mirror-like layer at the back of each eye that **reflects** light back into the eyes. This allows them to pick up all the light that there is.

A lion's eyes shine in the dark.

LIVING WITHOUT LIGHT

Deep underwater there is very little light. No plants can live down there. Deep-sea animals need large eyes to gather as much light as possible. Very few things live at the bottom of the ocean where there is no light at all.

On land the only place where it is ever truly dark is deep inside caves. Many cave animals have adapted to living without using their sight. Their eyes have become smaller over a long time. In some cases, they have disappeared completely.

Bats can see but are used to darkness. They live in dark caves and leave them only at night to hunt. Bats have a very well-developed sense of hearing. When flying, they make high-pitched squeaks and clicks. These sounds bounce (echo) off nearby objects, such as trees or insects. The bat can hear these echoes with its large ears. This is how it finds its way around and locates its **prey**.

A long-eared bat rests in the moonlight.

Making Light

Luminous Light

If you want to be active in the dark, one way is to make your own light. Some types of plants and animals can do this. They make a chemical light, which is a 'cold' light, rather than the hot light produced by most heat sources. This cold light is called **luminous light**.

The body of a glow-worm has chemicals that make light. The female glow-worm gives off a greenish glow at night to attract male glow-worms.

A glow-worm signals in the dark.

The deep-sea angler fish has a luminous lure on its head that it wiggles to look like a small lure. This attracts other fish who see the lure. As these fish come closer, they are sucked into the angler fish's huge mouth.

LIGHTING OUR WORLD

Most of our **artificial light** comes from burning things. In the past people used open flames as light. Candles, oil lamps and later, gas lamps were the only artificial sources of light for many years.

Thomas Edison made the first electric light in 1879. He passed an electric current through a thin carbon thread. This caused it to heat up and glow red-hot, giving off light. Electric lights have been developed a lot since then.

▶ *The light from a lightbulb comes from the glowing* **filament**.

LASER LIGHT

A **laser** is a machine that turns an ordinary beam of light into a very narrow beam of the brightest of bright light. Lasers have many uses. They can be used to cut metals. A laser beam slices through thick sheet steel as easily as a hot knife cuts through ice cream.

Lasers can create some of the most dazzling forms of night-time entertainment.

GLOSSARY

absorb (with light) the way colours are taken in by objects

artificial light light from devices made by humans

camouflage the colouring some animals have to keep them well-hidden

contact lenses lenses made of plastic or glass and worn in the eye to help a person see more clearly

filament thin wire that glows inside a light bulb

image picture made when light rays are reflected off a mirror, or bent through a lens

laser device that sends out a very bright beam of light

lens transparent object with curved sides that can focus light to make an image

luminous light light that is made by some plants and animals

nocturnal animal that is active at night and sleeps during the day

particles tiny parts of a substance

photosynthesis method by which plants make food using energy from the Sun

pollinate to move pollen from one flower to another

predators animals that live by hunting and eating other animals

prey animal that is hunted and eaten by other animals

prism triangular-shaped piece of glass that is used to reflect and refract light

pupil dark centre of the eye that lets light in

reflect bounce light back from a surface

reflection image made when light bounces back off a surface

refraction bending of light rays as they go from one material to another

retina part of the eye on which the image is formed

scattered light light rays spread out in all directions

translucent material that allows some light to pass through it

transparent material that allows nearly all light to pass through it

FURTHER INFORMATION

BOOKS

Light and Sound, Steve Parker (Hodder Wayland, 2000)

Light, Sound and Electricity, Kirsteen Rogers (Usborne, 2001)

My World of Science: Light and Dark, Angela Royston (Heinemann Library, 2001)

Science Experiments with Light, Sally Aston (Franklin Watts, 1999)

Smart Science: Sound and Light, Robert Snedden (Heinemann Library, 2000)

WEBSITES

Edison's Miracle of Light – learn about currents, lightbulbs, and batteries, get a timeline of Edison's life, hear historic recordings, and see a photo gallery. From American Experience on PBS.
http://www.pbs.org/wgbh/amex/edison

Explore Science – access a library of information on many science topics. Includes photos and artwork, video and animation, activities and tests.
http://www.heinemannexplore.com

Magic Factory – great games to teach you about basics of photography, including refraction, reflection, and the speed of light.
http://www.magic-factory.co.uk

The Speed of Light, – find out what light years are and how the speed of light is computed.
http://csep10.phys.utk.edu/guidry/violence/lightspeed.html

Unnatural Museum – Mirages – find out how light can play tricks with your eyes!
http://www.unmuseum.mus.pa.us/mirage.htm

INDEX